BURDENS LIFTED

Janet Walker

ARTHUR H. STOCKWELL LTD.
Torrs Park   Ilfracombe   Devon
Established 1898
www.ahstockwell.co.uk

British Library Cataloguing-in-Publication Data.
A catalogue record for this book is available
from the British Library.

Arthur H. Stockwell Ltd. bears no responsibility
for the accuracy of events recorded in this book.

By the same author:
My Journey with Jesus

ISBN 0-7223-3757-4
ISBN 978-0-7223-3757-8
Printed in Great Britain by
Arthur H. Stockwell Ltd.
Torrs Park   Ilfracombe
Devon

CONTENTS

SUE

Sue, my courageous friend:
Threads of colour,
As beautiful as her
Needlepoint
Ran through my life.

Her love for Jesus was
Real and down to earth,
With its ups and downs that all
Relationships go through.

Her deep friendship with Jesus
And all she new,
She valued more than words
Can say.

Sue, my courageous friend,
You will always be loved.

INTRODUCTION

This is the story of an ordinary person who had a journey within her relationship with Jesus.

It was a journey full of pain, joy, fear and peace, during which she was by turns labelled, understood, teased, loved, crushed, hugged, and encouraged.

When she was at school dyslexia was not particularly known about, but it caused problems with her reading, spelling, and maths. Frustration was a *big* part of her attempt to be able to do her schoolwork. Dyslexia played havoc with her piano-playing as for the left hand the notes seemed to be upside down.

She got to the age where she no longer believed she was what she had been called: thick and slow. The person who was creative, confident, persistent, that had battled with the other unconfident person, decided to do something about this. She plucked up courage and went to the doctor. He sent her to another doctor.

As she walked in and saw this older man, Father Christmas was brought to mind – it was the hair. As she sat down, before she knew it, out popped what she was thinking. His response was a big smile and, "Well, I've been called some things in my time, but that's a first."

An intense three hours was spent doing a range of tests. A week later she went back to a different doctor for the results, and she was told she was dyslexic and there was some ambidextrousness too. A letter could be written for any employer she may encounter if she so wished.

This thing that had played havoc for about twenty-two years now had a name.

This doctor seemed cold. Anger rose up inside her. "You're not reading a shopping list out, you know." Still more emotions popped out and, rightly or wrongly, she said, "You should go on a communication-skills course."

Time moved on. She never did use the letter for employers. Spelling continued to be the annoying factor; calculators helped with maths. Playing the piano using chords or a note here and there was a helpful substitute and meant she could gain pleasure from playing.

As time moved on she enjoyed her time working at the hospital, and met a wide variety of people. Life is full of variety because of people and all that they bring.

She did spend a short time with another employer, who was wonderful at encouraging her. He did this by allowing her to take phone messages. Her tummy would be in knots, but she became more confident at saying, "Please slow down. I can't write as quickly as you're talking." And somehow the manager was able to understand what had been written down by her.

She had thoughts, dreams and ambitions to be a doctor, vet, veterinary nurse, air hostess, hairdresser and an ice skater, all of which she knew would not come into being. Her deepest ambition, though, was to be a writer. She buried that deep inside in a make-believe wooden chest with a large lock, though her other thoughts might occasionally come out in front of friends. She later realised that her height would have been a problem if she had tried to become an air hostess, and she knew she would never acquire the necessary examination results for the other things.

Time moved on. She had gone to work as normal and had gone to get a roll from the canteen. As she was walking back an unusual pain came into her legs. It was quite unnerving. She got back to the unit by the skin of her teeth.

Later she came round on the bed in the office, and she had another two fits that afternoon.

That night she wrote to her longest-known friend in Australia and realised she was spelling words she thought she could not spell. Amazement, astonishment and joy filled her heart. To look up a word in the dictionary and find she had spelt it right was novel. It made her tingle all over.

There were another eight or so fits to come, over a period of time. Apprehension came with each fit. Would the greatly improved spelling be lost? There was never any medical explanation of why the fits happened.

She returned to work with spelling intact and continually improving, although she would still go blank sometimes. At such times fear and disbelief would come knocking at the door of her heart, but reassurance from Jesus and friends helped to improve this.

Time moved on, and 2002 came swiftly on its way. The corridor she had walked along so many, many times began to seem longer. As the days went on restlessness filled her mind and spirit in a way that it had never done before. September of that year came. Her last day was fast approaching. Much conversation and listening had gone on between her and Jesus. Was she willing to step out in faith and leave something she had known for over twenty years, to continue her journey knowing some of the things she would be doing, but only some?

The last day came. She had mixed feelings, and yet a powerful peace – a readiness. She knew in her heart that it was time to leave, and the great thing also was that she did not lose the friends she had made over that time. Her husband showed wonderful support also.

What was left of 2002 went very quickly. Unfortunately, after one week of leaving work, she needed time to get over the flu and time had to be spent resting. It was an opportunity to read, write letters and genuinely get on top of things slowly as the flu had taken the stuffing out of her.

Moving on, she spent nearly two years doing voluntary work, lending an ear if anyone needed to talk or pray something through. To listen to people is a precious and at times humbling experience.

She also started to write verse. This was something she had done many, many moons ago, as an outlet for strong feelings and thoughts at different times of her life. The poems were private and, if she is honest, they were nearly unreadable. The writing now came back as though they had never been apart; the difference this time was that it was readable.

This particular day her friend popped round. It was a lovely warm day, so the friend made herself comfortable in the garden while she made some cold drinks. While doing this she asked Jesus for confirmation about what she thought He had been placing on her heart, which was writing a book of verse and getting it published.

This lady sat with her drink enjoying the sunshine. She was then given what had been written so far. When she had finished reading the verses she put them on her lap, and said, "You should get them published. Have you written any more?"

Later that day Jesus reminded her about the wooden chest and the dream of a little girl. The time had come to open the chest. A magazine, which she had been getting for about five years, had an advert for new authors, including poets. She had never noticed it before because she had always skipped those pages. The answer to her question – Who should I send it to? – was in those pages.

One of the places she had done her volunteer work was at a lovely coffee and book shop, the other wonderful aspect of having her book published was that she was reunited with friends that she had not seen for about fifteen years. They played (and continue to play) a vital role, by having the book on the counter, along with their love and support for her as a person.

All that was needed for the little book to come into being happened. She watched and waited as things unfolded and came to be.

Jesus also gave her the courage to book a room at her local venue, with the support of her husband, to hold a book signing. When she went to acquire some card for the invitations, she had the right amount of money in her purse. On the day of the signing she experienced amazing love and support.

You, the reader, will dip into bits of her (my) life. Some things have been shared; some have not.

None of what you read was or is meant to be pretentious. Sometimes to share my story, means a person who has caused me pain and unhappiness, and vice versa, will have to come into the picture because I'm not writing an imaginary story.

As you dip into pockets of my life, I hope Jesus will shine through me. He sheared, sewed up, restored me and gave me the ability to forgive against the odds. He never gave up on me; He hated the sin but continued to love me. He saw potential, cried with me through other people, and when I was on my own I felt His invisible arms around me.

And those people that know me and what my laugh is like can surely be in no doubt that Jesus has got a sense of humour.

WRATH

Wrath is a word not commonly used in today's society. The dictionary definition of wrath is great anger. We all have different situations in our lives that at times can cause us great anger. One of mine is seeing a gravestone that has been vandalised.

The word wrath is also found in some of the older Bibles, which also have words like thy, thou and thee.

The Bible is full of emotions. I personally find all the different people, struggling with themselves, others and their relationships with Jesus, quite a comfort. They help me not to feel so alone, because, like any relationship, it's not always easy.

The word wrath has a lot of energy in some ways. As we know, anger is a powerful force that if not controlled can cause mayhem and destruction to ourselves and others. Sometimes it's a bit like an onion, which looks a bit yellow on the outside, but when you get to the core it's gone rotten.

I remember a teacher at my secondary school who would show my work up in front of the class. I wanted the ground to open up and let me fall through it. Anger would well up inside me, and every time I saw this lady in the corridor another nibble of anger would burst through. The ingredients of embarrassment, anger and frustration would lead me to the headmistress's room, to ask her to have a word with this teacher. If the headmistress was available, a green light would come on, and in I would go. More than often, to my dismay, the green light would not light up and I would have to try again later. When I was successful, there did seem to be a slight change in this teacher, for a short period of time.

Unforgivingness and anger are not a good combination. Probably the better way to have handled that situation would have been to meet with the teacher herself and explain why I found the subject so hard, and to have asked her if she could help me in some way to overcome the difficulty. Clarity and understanding are very important ingredients in such (or should I say all?) situations.

If I had done the above, I would have forgiven her much more quickly, and the pain that was being caused would have been sorted out, along with the anger.

Jesus helped me a long time ago with this and other episodes in my life.

WRATH AND US

Sometimes confusion can reign when it comes to God, wrath and anger. I'm no academic, but I feel God has something to say about this. Do you feel love and wrath don't go together? And yet when you love someone it does not mean you wouldn't get angry with them – even *very* angry at times. We all have little idiosyncrasies – quirks within our personalities. One of mine, which at times drives my friends up the wall, is when I interrupt them. The trouble is, I'm so into what they're saying that my mind goes into gear, and my response comes before they've had a chance to finish the sentence. Just think, the tongue is so small, but my! does it need the brake on sometimes.

When you love a child and you know fire can be dangerous, you know it needs to be treated with respect; so you lovingly tell the child not to get too near or don't touch the end of the sparkler. It's hot and you get burnt fingers. Curiosity and naughtiness leads to burnt fingers and tears – all the things you wanted to avoid. Unfortunately the child can think you're being a spoilsport by saying no. And yet all you wanted was for them to feel no pain. Then their curiosity and naughtiness can drive you to despair and impatience, and you can feel completely dried out. You still love the child, but don't necessarily like their actions.

God's dislike of sin is real. My dislike of memorials being vandalised is real. Perhaps a couple will have had a seat placed in what was their favourite park, where they spent happy times together, and then for them to find it's been vandalised will be so upsetting.

Sin is another kettle of fish, in the sense that it separates us from Father God. We all enjoy or have, hopefully, enjoyed different types of relationship: girlfriend, boyfriend, gran, auntie, uncle, friend. We were created to be in relationships; the very first one, though, is to

11

be in a relationship with Father God. And – personally, I feel – nothing can replace that space. You can love someone a great deal – however, they cannot get inside you, they cannot get inside your soul, and we are mind, body and soul! Sometimes I can't find the words to express what I am feeling deep down inside. It's as though there are no words to describe the feeling, and, with the best will in the world, your friend can't get inside you and into your soul, despite loving you loads. That space, that feeling, that need is not being met.

When we feel low or down we don't always know why. A shopping spree or holiday is a good quick fix, but because we're separated from the ingredient that can deal with "Why do I feel like this?" it means going back to the person that we were supposed to have that first relationship with – Jesus.

One day I was cycling home from work. As I was cycling down the main road a car hit me sideways on. Amazingly I went up in the air, landed on top of the car that had hit me, rolled down past the windscreen onto the bonnet, then hit the road and landed outside a pub.

The doctor, the nurses and myself were astonished that I had not ended up under the car. I was extremely fortunate to have also landed on the car while it was still moving.

Amazingly no bones were broken. I was just badly bruised on one hip, had a bit of delayed shock, and needed a new bike. The driver was taken off the road, because this time they made contact, so to speak. It must have been a terribly shock for my parents to see my friend standing on their doorstep with my mangled bike. He was also on his way home that night, and happened to be behind the lorry that was behind me.

When my parents arrived at the hospital, I was waiting to have an X-ray. As you can see, I got off very lightly.

In a way, the person tried to separate me from my bike, the road, and getting home that night; sin will try and separate you from God, so you lose out on a amazing relationship.

Oh, my! I am going to be bold and say, "Why should God not get angry?" For a moment I was angry when that driver went into me. For those few moments I couldn't believe my eyes, and I remember saying very quickly, "Jesus, help me." But also I was angry at the same time.

He gets angry and upset at the things that separate us from Him,

12

just as we can really love someone but at the same time still become angry with them. We don't stop loving the person, but that does not necessarily mean we won't feel angry if they hurt or reject us.

At different times in our lives we all feel different depths of anger, so why not God? I feel He is much better at dealing with anger than we can be. Sometimes we have to say No in a relationship – it might break our hearts, but love needs to be tough sometimes.

God said no more separation, so He sent Jesus as the sacrifice. Jesus took all our sin, pain, rubbish, sorrow and anger, and nailed them to a cross so we could come into a relationship with the Father God and Jesus. And, by rising on the third day, Jesus really did the Evil One's head in, because Jesus took away his greatest weapon – death!

Father God practised tough love, by letting His Son come and be the sacrifice for the rubbish. And Jesus practised tough love by going through with it.

To do the above and still get rejected by people must cause Father God and Jesus pain beyond belief.

Wrath is real, because God the Father is real and His Son Jesus Christ is real, just as our anger or wrath is real. The difference is that ours – mine – unless it's nipped in the bud can do so much more damage to us and those around us. A righteous anger will always have at its core the ability to be wise and moral – something I cannot always manage, but God the Father and His Son can!

COMRADESHIP

Comradeship is a wonderful emotion to experience, especially when it threads its way through a relationship. I went to a boarding school for the second part of my secondary-school life, and I was part of a group of twenty day girls. Comradeship was very important to both the boarders and the day girls.

Unfortunately there was a lot of hostility between the two groups. This always caused me great sadness. I so wanted the comradeship to be among us, as one group of people. In so many ways I could understand why the boarders felt as they did: they saw us go home at the end of each day.

One day my friend was being picked on. I was worried for her. The person picking on her could be quite rough. Later that day this girl and I were alone in the corridor, and, probably for the first time in my life, I tried to be assertive, controlled and loving. I had a go at explaining that just because we go home after school didn't mean everything was brilliant, and it didn't mean we had no problems within our own families. So, I said, instead of being jealous and spiteful, let's support each other – after all, school and, for some, home life was tough enough. The last thing either group needed was bullying. Things did improve after that, but like all relationships there was always room for improvement.

Then during the last year or so it was really put to the test when I was made a prefect. Being a prefect and a day girl really didn't go down very well. I tried to explain when needed (which at the time seemed often!) that I had not volunteered for this role. Nobody likes to put himself into a venerable position unnecessarily. I had been picked and that was that.

Spending time at this school taught me a lot about myself and other people, and it taught me that at times you have to stick up for yourself, comrades, and your relationship with Jesus. The other thing we had in common was poor self-image. This showed itself in different ways in each person.

Before going to the boarding school, I had to decide whether to stay were I was and struggle, or go to a school that in some ways I knew would be too easy. So, in tears, I turned to Jesus as a thirteen-year-old because I just didn't know what to do. And so the boarding school was to be the one. When the pupils in my class realised I was going to a school with no homework and a swimming pool they all thought, 'Lucky old you.' There were days when I thought, 'Oh, Lord, why this school?' but with hindsight I would not have coped where I was, and I would not have met such a diverse lot of people – and yet they were so similar in some ways. Also I was lucky to have people encourage me in my poor swimming ability, and in turn I was able to encourage them back.

So the Lord Jesus did show me the correct school, and through the difficulties, along with the good times, my relationship with Jesus and other people grew.

While I continued to grow through the teenage years, life continued to be a bit like a roller-coaster ride. And you could say Jesus represented the safety bar. But unlike a roller-coaster ride, where you need to be a certain height otherwise you cannot go on the ride, Jesus fits all sizes. He is more interested in your inner self than your outer self. We are bombarded by society trying to sell us every anti-wrinkle cream going, shampoo for every type of hair condition, and spot cream – though when I was a teenager there was less choice, which made the buying of these products easier. The great thing about having a relationship with Jesus is that He is available twenty-four hours a day. He sees me at my best and my worst – the days when I'm running late or lazy days when it's a quick under-the-arm job. Thank goodness for body sprays!

When I asked Jesus into my life and heart, we didn't just start a relationship – He took residence in my soul. He helped me along the way by showing me that a lot of what we feel is by our emotions. We might see, hear, smell, touch, and then react, but still our language can let us down. You can't find the words yourself, let alone explain to your friends how you're feeling, but Jesus can get inside those unexplainable feelings. It's really great to be able to have this type of intimacy in the relationship; also, sometimes it has to be spirit to spirit, not flesh to flesh.

Our minds play a important role alongside our emotions. However, I personally find my emotions will try and overrule what my mind will be trying to stay focused on. Here is an example of this: Every other week I play the guitar, and lead some songs at my friend's house. I need to focus my mind on the guitar chords and be sensitive to how Jesus is moving within the group. One night my husband turned into our road as I was coming out. His food was already prepared for him, which would save time and would mean he could join us shortly. Time went on and he seemed a long time coming. My mind was thinking, 'Where is he? Has someone phoned?' The emotions that were accompanying those thoughts were taking over to such a point that I lost where I was musically and ended up singing a different verse to everyone else. The song came to a stop as I realised I was the only one singing.

GARDENS

When it comes to gardens, I take after my dad. Whether visiting a garden or looking after our own, we would be in our element. With a garden, whatever its size, hard work usually pays off, and hopefully gives pleasure – even if it's only a window box, a dash of colour can really brighten your day. My favourite plants are roses, the only problem is the constant fight against black leaf, and all the other problems associated with that particular plant. Bluebells are much easier – if they appear in your garden they take care of themselves, and smell brilliant too. I had some pink bluebells come up one year in my garden; they had the most wonderful pastel shade of pink, and a delicate complexity that was a beautiful sight to behold.

Jesus will put a lot of work into trying to gain your attention. I had a friend who was very persistent, and every Sunday she would ask me to go with her to Sunday school. Her class was called Jucos. So one Sunday I said yes, and I'm ashamed to say I only said yes because she was driving me up the wall. This friend showed determination, patience, and love in her conquest to introduce me to Jesus, who she knew could and does get angry, but will not have vindictiveness and malice at the core. She wanted me to meet for myself this person, Jesus, who loved her unconditionally. She had found someone who loved her for who she was – quirks and all.

Within a few weeks of going to Jucos I started to see love in action. We were so fortunate in having a lovely teacher, who was very patient, kind and understanding, and had incredible listening skills. Her life had not always been easy; also her relationship with her sister was very similar to mine (chalk and cheese). I really felt I could relate to this person/teacher. Her love for Jesus was so strong and yet she was so down-to-earth. I just got to the point where I thought I would rather have Jesus on the inside than the outside. I remember that it was with great joy that I told my friend and teacher that I had accepted Jesus into my heart and life; and I thanked my friend for her persistence. I also admitted to her why I'd given in and gone with her all those months ago.

So, just like all the hard work you have to put into a garden, my friend's hard work – and love! – for me, along with a lot of urging, encouragement, work, and energy, Jesus would have done through her and with her to get my attention.

As mentioned before, this did not stop the roller-coaster ride, but by asking Him into my heart and life I found out for myself that He really does fit all sizes.

BALLROOM DANCING

As a family we all enjoyed ballroom dancing, each person taking part and acquiring bronze, silver, and gold awards. If done properly it can feel like you're gliding across the floor. There was a lovely gentleman whom I would have the pleasure of dancing with if I went in the evening. There was a ladies' invitation, where you went and asked the man of your choice to dance. At the time, one of my favourite dances was the foxtrot; as soon as the ladies' invitation for the foxtrot was announced I was off to my gentleman and inviting him to dance with me. He always said yes, bless him! He would stand and bow and I would curtsey. All too quickly the dance would be over. He always finished with a bow, and in return I would curtsey. On a Saturday my sister, Mum, and myself would go down and get the room and floor ready for the children and young people, who would fill the ballroom.

I must admit I loved being there before all the crowd came in. One of my jobs was to sprinkle wax on the floor to stop people slipping over. When I first started doing this the bucket was nearly as big as I was. It's no wonder they called me Little 'Un and Half Pint. Since then some more names have been added: Mischief, Trouble, Sweetheart. . . . Then before you knew it the doors would open and in they would all come. It was a bit like a stampede. The first ten to fifteen minutes or so I would find difficult; being shy and timid made the need to run and hide quite powerful, but I could never seem to get out to the toilets before the stampede, so to speak. My other job was to rally the children and get them up dancing. This was also a nightmare. I'm sure this was to build my confidence up, but when you're young you don't quite see it like that.

Because of this, your outlook on life can be different to that of your parents, and a word here and there can leave scars which need to be dealt with later. I remember one day a member of my family had gone down to collect my results for my gold medal, and I was told I had been given a 'commended'. The set-up for medals was: pass, commended, and highly commended. For bronze and silver I had been given a pass. They were so astonished, they checked the results again. In all honesty, I was totally astonished myself. Sometimes, though, we need someone to say, "Well done!" and perhaps not look so surprised when giving the information. The astonishment they showed at my achievement was very painful at the time, even though I'm sure they did not consciously wish to cause me pain. Unfortunately, though, the pain will nibble away at your emotions, and harm your self-image. I suppose, rightly or wrongly, you hope that others will not be as astonished as you – that you can do better than you thought possible.

SHOWS AND RELATIONSHIPS

My sister took part in different shows and talent competitions. One show was *The Sound of Music*. It was a family favourite. I would sing quietly under my breath. After the show you could go backstage for refreshments. We never did quite manage it, and I was never courageous enough to say to my parents that I felt my sister might like us to follow the performances through by going backstage and meeting the cast and spending time with her. In this instance it was not about how my parents would react, it was more about how I would react, feel, think, if it did not go down well as a suggestion. Since then, I've learnt that, however you or the person might react, the opportunity might only be there for a moment and so you've just got to go for it.

From the age of thirteen, when I started my relationship with Jesus, music and dance had become important avenues to channel the stress and frustration I would feel at times. So in many ways it was really great that, like my friend, I had found in Jesus someone that loved me, quirks and all – someone who knew me better than I knew myself. He saw the private tears – the tears that were there but wouldn't come out. He saw and felt every hidden pain. He struggled with me and shared my anxiety and discouragement, along with the joy of the foxtrot with the lovely gentleman, a piano and guitar. Also people would come into my life just at a time that was perfect timing for where I was, whether it be spiritually, mentally, or emotionally. Jesus did not spare me the emotion anger, and yet deep down I knew His correcting of me was part of our relationship; and, even though I was young, I just knew it was correction done within a love that was uncompromising, and within a love without the complications of human frailty – myself included in that frailty.

ELSE

As I was growing up there was another lady who came into my life, who was a strength and an inspiration. I am sure I was with her from a young age. She would look after me when Mum was at work. I soon started calling her Auntie Else, and it was a name that stuck. She was fine about me calling her by that name. From about the age of eight I would go and spend Sunday afternoons with her. We would sit and have a chat or watch the Sunday afternoon black-and-white matinee. Then it would be time for the big brown teapot, bread, butter, and cheese. She would cut a lovely thick slice from the loaf of bread, then – the best bit – we would put a toasting fork through the bread, and hold it over the coal fire. The butter would melt, along with the cheese, soon after spreading; then, as you bit into it, the bread was so soft your nose would disappear into the butter and cheese. What a sight! As you can imagine, tissues were an essential part of the afternoon – so was blowing your nose afterwards. It was great. We would just laugh with each other and have endless cups of tea out of the *big* brown teapot. I don't know if it was because I was young, but to me it was the best toast ever. I'm sure the coal dust added to the taste. This lady was not always in good health and yet her life was full, helping to run a business, which for her was a lot of washing. She did not have the luxury of a washing machine, but my! could she get the overalls white. I would go every Sunday – and in the week too if I could – until I left my hometown.

When I went to visit my dad I would go and see Auntie Else, who now lived in a residential nursing home. One day I had gone down with my boyfriend to see Dad and went to visit Auntie Else, but in between visits she had died. There are no words to describe what I felt like, except perhaps numb. She had been such a precious part of my growing up. I came out feeling numb. I couldn't speak. I sat on the wall, too numb to cry. I also learnt that day, again, how important communication is: my boyfriend just took one look at me when I got back to my dad's and seemed to know not to ask how the visit had gone. Sadly, I had never really communicated to my dad how much this lady really meant to me, how grateful I was that she had lived so near to us, or how grateful I was for her friendship, for her companionship, for our Sunday afternoons. Lack of information to my dad over the years about this, made it difficult for him to understand that part of me had died with her. He knew I loved the parks in our town. There is a beautiful one that has a beautiful lake and lovely grounds. It must have been awful for my boyfriend and Dad as we walked around the park. The pain of loss was acute. I was grateful to Dad for suggesting we went to the park, but unfortunately I was aware I was walking in a daze and when spoken to could only answer with very few words.

People might find it hard to believe I could be a person of few words, especially as, at the time and since, my nickname was and has been Chatterbox – however, inner pain can have that impact on you to be quiet.

HAIRDRESSING

Cutting hair and nails has been a fascination for me as long as I can remember.

I was always offering to cut anybody's hair that would let me, but I never had any takers – I wonder why? – so dolls that had long hair came in very handy. I also liked cars, and my favourite was double-decker buses – however, the desire to get snipping was never very far away.

So when I started my first hairdressing apprenticeship I was over the moon. The shop was a nice size – not too big. I made the third person. The till did not add up for you and tell you how much change to give, and I must admit my whole attention was taken up with wanting to learn how to be a hairdresser. Maths and English had never been my strong point, so answering the phone, having to write people's names down for an appointment, and giving change scared the living daylights out of me. The things I would get up to to avoid answering the phone or giving change! "Oh, I need the toilet," came in useful (again). The manageress put it down to nerves, which was true in a way, but the acute embarrassment of not being able to spell or deal with change played a large part in my wishing to visit the toilet. My! I've seen a lot of toilets in my time. I employed other ideas to dodge facing them (honest!). One day, though, it all came to a head and I gave a lady the wrong change. The next day the manageress had words with me. With tears, out it all came. There were wise words from her. At the time I thought, 'No, thank you. I don't want to face this. It's too painful and frustrating,' but she still gently insisted that I answer the phone and give change. She would try and give me ladies who would not mind, or who would not make me feel embarrassed if I asked for their help in giving them the correct change, or if the phone went and I had to ask how to spell their name. Most days butterflies would accompany me, and change their ferocity with what was going on in the day. Jesus came to my aid with the difficulty of giving change. On our side of the road there were three houses, and the third one was split into two flats. In the bottom flat there was a lovely lady whom I got on very well with. Jesus urged me to go and see her and share the problems I was having at the hairdressers, which I did. After a hug, some tears, and a cup of tea she went and got her tin of money. I took some of the money and we then played shop for hours. It made such a vast difference at the shop. I'm so glad Jesus encouraged me to go to my friend.

NEGATIVE AND POSITIVE

As it turned out I did not fulfil my apprenticeship at this hairdresser's. Sadly, there were things that went on, which meant I was given my notice, but as it turned out it was not a bad thing. I did not feel comfortable about certain things that were going on within the shop, but I had been willing to put up with them because I wanted to be a hairdresser.

My time there had not been wasted, though. Issues that I had not wanted to face for a long time – my spelling and maths – had to be faced, because now I was dealing with the public, not children and young teens who struggled with the same issues as I did, or teachers and house mothers who were trying to help a large group of children and teens with emotional, physical, and mental problems.

My disappointment, frustration, sadness and anger ran quite deep – not particularly towards the shop, as I was not the first to be given notice. To this day, though, I wish I had done something about it – I don't know what, just something.

I was angry, puzzled, and resentful towards Jesus because this had happened, and yet at the same time grateful that He had urged me to go to my friend with the problem of giving change. It was a strange position to be in, having such strong feelings. My relationship with Jesus was and is very real and down to earth; the combination of disappointment, frustration, anger, sadness, resentfulness, along with the love, admiration, respect, and deepness of relationship with Jesus was quite a position to be in.

Jesus gently but firmly reminded me that hanging on to the above emotions would nibble away at me. To feel them and experience them was not unusual – nobody likes being fired unfairly. He understood why I was angry with Him, but He also reminded me what had been achieved, apart from the giving of change and asking the clients how to spell their names, such as learning to cope with different types of personality with the children and teens. I'd met people from all walks of life at this hairdresser's which continued the learning curve I'd begun with the children, teens and myself at the boarding school. Reminding me of these facts helped me to see it from His perspective; which then helped me to give Him the strong emotions I was feeling and let Him bring something positive out of a negative situation.

STEAMROLLER

The plans we sometimes have for ourselves are not necessarily the correct ones, especially as we cannot always see the bigger picture. I did try once more at another hairdresser's, but it did not work out there either. I've never known the Lord to waste experiences. What I learnt at both hairdresser's would come in very handy later, in different situations that I could not have known at the time would come into being.

I don't know about you, but I was and can still be a bit like a steamroller. Sometimes when I was young I would go to the park and watch a man push a big iron roller over the grass, so it was completely flat for the game of bowls that would take place later that day. I was fascinated by the size of this thing. It looked so big and heavy, though sometimes the guy pushing it was not exactly muscular. He had the patience to walk up and down over and over again, and he did his job properly so that the people playing the game would get more pleasure out of the game. In a way you could say he saw the bigger picture. He was the unseen part of the game, but he was just as important as the players, just as Jesus could see I only needed to learn what I had learnt so that later I could be part of the game team. Like that man with the roller, what at times must have been tedious was actually a very important part of the whole game. Sometimes I (we) need to be the complete opposite to a steamroller. Also, on those afternoons I saw with my own eyes the importance of patience. The green always looked so much better for all the hard work, just as, in the same way, the patience Jesus showed me paid off, even if sometimes it was later rather than sooner on my part.

Waiting and being patient all too often seem to go together. I remember the few hours between the main Christmas presents and the tree presents. When you're young those few hours seem for ever. I suppose it would help matters if you didn't keep looking at the clock. I just could not see how having a gap in the middle would help you appreciate the first lot of presents and let your dinner go down. No way – let's get ripping (steamroller) – after all, the tree presents were chocolate money, sweets, and fruit. Brilliant! More food! I was like a stick to look at, but my! I could eat for England. I had hollow legs (no change there). The rest between the two lots of presents was good, if only for the sake of my tummy, so you could say parents need to be cruel to be kind at times. Prevention is better than having to learn the hard way, but sometimes the only way we learn is the hard way. Not letting me into the tree presents prevented my eating too much at once and prevented me feeling or being sick.

Jesus often tries to prevent me having to learn the hard way, but if I choose not to listen, like all decisions there are consequences.

DENTIST

The consequence of not saying something to the person concerned is not always good. This episode happened many moons ago, but I feel it is something that should be shared.

Teeth had always been a problem for me, just as they can be for other people. I had very strong roots attached to my baby teeth. The teeth in the front of my mouth did not want to fall out of their own accord, so the adult teeth started to grow along the inside of the gum. Because I had had a fair number of operations on my ears I was as used to going into hospital as anyone can be, and I usually knew what to expect with those operations — the unknown. I looked like I'd been in a boxing ring with Mike Tyson. Also, the awful thing afterwards, apart from the pain, was my breath. I could smell it was bad without anyone saying anything. I got through a lot of mouthwash tablets.

Later I had to have a brace on my top teeth to push everything together. It was called a cemented brace. It was ugly and sharp and took a long time to put in.

The morning arrived. The chap seemed nice and he was aware I was nervous. There was much talking to Jesus whenever I went to the dentist. I had always hated the thought, and this day was no exception. To begin with the dental nurse stayed in, which was comforting, and I must admit every time she went out I felt panic inside though I did not know why at first.

I was not a big-breasted person, but as the procedure went on he started to rest his arm on my breast. I felt really uncomfortable about this. I knew the treatment was going to last a least an hour. Inside I was panicking. I did not want to be alone with this guy. I prayed over and over again for the dental nurse to come back, and she did. My part was to say something to her, or him while she was there, even if it was to please hold his arm so it was not on my breast; to hand him what he needs so he does not take them off the tissue which is lying on the other breast; or even to say to him, while she was there, to stop. Every time she went out the feelings intensified. She came back in, so now would be a good time to be a chatterbox, or push him off, but it was as though the mechanism in my tongue and arm had stopped working. The consequence of not saying anything was that inside I was screaming, "Get off!"

Afterwards he said, "Was everything OK?" and again I was nearly speechless and said, "Yes." My inner self was angry, which produced adrenalin, which should have helped me to say, "No! Actually, when I come in again if your arm gets tired you call for a nurse and *do not* touch my chest!"

I was given many opportunities to speak up, and I had many urges from Jesus to say how I was feeling. I had to make a decision about the treatment I was being given, to heed the opportunities and urges to say something, or suffer the consequences of saying nothing and feel as though my head would explode from the inside. I had been given the resources to change what was happening.

DENTIST AND CONSEQUENCES

At every new appointment I was given more opportunities to say something. I am sure it must have been heartbreaking for Father God to see what this guy was doing. You might say "Why didn't He intervene?" but I feel He did. He is respectful of my will and was trying to encourage me to stand up for myself. If He had intervened any more than He did, I would not have grown – I would have stayed stunted as a plant will if not watered or nourished enough. We sometimes need to put some effort in ourselves. Without that experience I would not understand how awful someone feels when they do not want to be touched, or realise I needed to do something about learning to stand up for myself. I had to learn not to let timidity keep my mouth shut when I need to say something; not to let insecurity of self allow someone to make me feel dirty.

From my relationship point of view with Father God and His Son Jesus I learnt you never cry alone; by the power of the Holy Spirit I felt invisible arms round me, whether I was crying inwardly or outwardly. I also learnt that He will do everything but say it for you, because He knows it's something you've got to do yourself. It's like a toddler who will keep falling over while learning to walk – if you don't let the child fall he wouldn't get up and try again. Even though there might be tears, intervening too much would stop the child learning how to walk (tough love).

In that episode I certainly learnt what the consequences can be to circumstances. And I learnt to appreciate people's space, and so to this day I will try to read their body language to understand if they would be a person that would want a hug. I have often failed, especially in my early years, and even after the dentist episode. However, hopefully time has improved things.

Over the years, Jesus has shown me what to share with people.

I can try to explain that deep physical, emotional and mental inner hurts can really be helped the most by Jesus. Because the pain can be so deep, the healing has to be done by someone who can get inside your pain with you. There can be a big difference in the body language of someone not wanting a hug from you, and, if misread, this can be painful for you and suffocating for them. I have experienced occasions where people have gone over the line with me, and the different depths of pain that can cause is one of life's consequences; however, I hope that letting you into a piece of my past will help you know you are not alone.

MOTHER-IN-LAW

I have been fortunate enough to have had two lovely mothers-in-law. The first lady had a real mixed bag for a daughter-in-law, but kindly let me into a loving relationship with her and took me on as her daughter and friend. She would stand up for me in front of her son or husband if she felt it was needed.

We both had a dog. My dog was called Shandy; unfortunately I cannot remember the name of hers. One day her son and I took Shandy over to meet his mum and let the two dogs meet. That day she came home from work to find two dogs sitting next to each other, one looking very pleased to see Mum. Then Shandy dived for cover behind my legs. The dear lady just seemed to take it in her stride and made Shandy feel very welcome too. I knew Shandy was happy as she fell asleep on the lady's lap as we had a cup of tea.

One Christmas they all found out how much I hate games, especially board games. This lady was completely the opposite and found them very enjoyable. This year after dinner she made it very clear that the television was out and family time was going to happen around the table. This is not bad in itself – a cup of tea or coffee and a chat, yes, but not games. I desperately tried to get out of doing this. I am sure pure panic makes my mind go blank and the rules of the game always seem beyond me. You know what it's like when someone says, "Does everyone understand?" and everyone says "Yes," and your mouth seems to be sealed up with superglue. Or in a group setting they might say, "Put your hand up," and your arm becomes like a dead weight. Embarrassment takes over and you sit there dreading your turn.

This day was no exception. We started to go round the table, and much too quickly it was my turn. I bluffed my way through the first round – however, increasingly, my emotional state was near to exploding. My throat was hurting as I was desperately trying not to cry. My turn arrived again. The father became inpatient with me. Tears flooded out. I ran and hid in her son's bedroom with him in hot pursuit. The pent-up frustration came out in near-hysterical tears. His mum arrived and tried to calm me down. She was at first mystified about why I was so upset, but after a while, with me a bit calmer, out it all came. From that day if I said I would rather read or watch television in the sitting room while they played games, she was OK with this. As time went on I sometimes watched while they played, but was not forced to join in, or I would sometimes play with her son if I understood how to play the game.

Sadly, my relationship with her son did not work out, and later we were divorced. This was very sad as I lost a good friend in this lady. She showed such grace in the situation, and, by having words with her son, she was the means of my having the money that was owed to me later on in the divorce.

One day we bumped into each other, and I said how sad I was that things had not worked out between her son and me, and she said, "It takes two to make a marriage, and as much as I love my son I know he is not perfect."

Before we parted we gave each other a hug, and as we did this I thanked her for her friendship and hoped she could forgive me for the part I played in the failed marriage. I did see her again some years later when I thought her son and I were going to be getting back together, but after a while he made it *very* clear that this was not going to happen.

Jesus showed me years later that He can and does mend the broken-hearted.

It was my first day at school and we all sat on little coloured chairs. Even then pink and yellow were the colours I liked. We all sat round in a circle on those little coloured chairs. I tipped mine backwards to balance on the back legs, and got away with it for a while, but then to my dismay the chair fell back with me doing a full flip. I ended up caught on the chair, with that day's washing on view for everyone to see. I vaguely remember my pants might have been the same colour as the chair I had been sitting on. The children thought this very funny – especially the boys. Sorry, guys! The teacher seemed to take an absolute age in coming to my rescue so that I could sit down again. The poor teacher was finding it very difficult not to laugh, but could see I was mortified. Even though I was very young, and did not have a clue what the words would have been to say how I was feeling, I just knew I did not like what I was feeling inside.

Now I can see the funny side of that particular incident, but my! it was not funny at the time. To this day I won't rock in a chair, and if I see someone doing this and they go flying, I sometimes remember my pink-chair incident and thank God that I can laugh. However, it was an inner embarrassment that I was very happy for Jesus to heal. It was such a long time ago, but I had to learn that it had stuck and made a difference to anything that involved being in a circle or even a group. This was made clear over time, and the game that Christmas with my first in-laws was the beginning of this realisation.

As I said, I am grateful for that inner healing and I cope quite differently now with games and can laugh with people. There might be a few butterflies, but the difference now between not wanting to do them because I'm not bothered and not wanting to because I'm terrified is quite a difference.

COLOURS AND THE GUITAR

Colours, shades, and depths of pastel colours have always fascinated me, from the beautiful deep rustic amber, gold, orange and red on a changing autumn leaf, to the reflection on a lake or a mountain capped with snow. My favourite colours are pastel shades of pink, yellow and violet, but the colours mentioned above are not far behind.

My first guitar was definitely chosen for its shade of dark red. It was hanging near the top of the room in the music shop with its back showing. It really stood out. (Most of the other guitars were different shades of brown.) I still have it today. On this guitar I had my first guitar lesson. Learning to play the guitar is very hard on the fingers, so surgical spirit came in handy for helping to make the skin hard. It was a tip from the teacher, just to put a little on the end of the fingers till the skin got more used to pushing on the strings. The other good way to harden your fingers is to practise. I did not mind practising, but I still seemed to be struggling to keep up with the others. Patience, determination and persistence were required and prayers were uttered. The teacher was lovely; so was her helper, who kindly gave me extra help at home.

Every year we would do a concert. There were three groups: beginners, intermediates, and advanced. We all took part, and our group would play things together or in twos. I got on very well with a girl who was the same age as me, and sometimes in these concerts we would play together. One year we played and sang along with an Abba song which went down very well. My piano teacher made it that year, which was great. The concerts were only once a year so we were all very happy! The lights were down in the room, so we couldn't see people looking at us; and as we were beginners we always went first.

Some years later I was to find out why I had learnt to be patient and determined while I was learning the guitar. The helper and I stayed friends. Early one evening she turned up on my doorstep and asked me to bring my guitar. At first I wanted to know why and I was not keen to go with her until I had more information. However, she knew me well and knew that if she told me more I would have run a mile. There was a school that had its gym in a separate building, and it was just up the road from where I lived. In the end I agreed to go with her to see what she was so eager to show me.

We walked into the gym, and sitting there were three groups of children and young teens. She pointed to a group and said, "They're yours." For a moment I was speechless. She said, "They're the beginners. I've put some songs over there ready."

Before I found my voice I found my legs, and before she could stop me I had done a runner, with thoughts racing through my mind like 'You must be joking!' She could also run fast and soon caught me up. I said I could understand she needed help teaching, but not me – please, not me. I had never done any teaching, and my being quite deaf in one ear would make it hard for me to hear my group because of the noise from the others.

My legs had turned to jelly by this point and I sincerely thought I would be more of a hindrance than a help to her. In the end – bless her! – she said, "Please, just have a go, at least for tonight." So off we went, and as we were walking these words came to my mind: 'Be courageous. With me all things are possible.'

With this in mind in we walked. I had about six children in my group. The only song I can remember out of the two left on the chair was 'Puff the Magic Dragon'. It has very few chords in it, which is most helpful when you're first learning, and this is helpful from a teaching perspective too. I then found out it's one thing to sing with someone, but to sing on your own is a different kettle of fish altogether, and it was especially hard to sing in front of children who say what they think. We got started and it was not long before they started to say (and rightly so), "We can't hear you."

I need to sidetrack for a moment: During different times, due to my poor hearing, I would speak or laugh at a level that was just right for my amount of hearing but would be too loud for other people. They would say "Could you tone it down a bit?" or they would say it with their body language, without saying a word, so I was continuously trying to do this. But at this particular time, when others were concentrating on their group and probably would not have noticed the volume coming from me, I still found singing and getting the volume right for my group hard. There was a hour to fill with these children and I was concerned it might get boring for them, but ideas came through and the time went quite quickly. Then, before I knew it, I gave them some things to practise and said, "See you next week." Then, after a few moments I realised what I had said. My friend also heard what I had said and was well pleased. I must admit at this point I was not sure if it would work, and told her how the lesson had gone, but she said would I consider giving it a few more goes?

She said she could always move my group a little further away, so with this in mind I agreed to have a go.

As the weeks passed it became clear quite early on that most of the children in my group were struggling in the same way I had, so my empathy with how they were feeling was real. I found I really enjoyed teaching, and the rapport became very good between us as a group. I really didn't mind how slowly the song was done or how many times I needed to put their fingers in the right place.

A foundation was set in those years with the children. I learnt a lot about what can be achieved as an individual and with a team; my faith and trust within my relationship with Jesus improved, and again His timing was perfect. Sharing the joy of learning with the children and watching the joy on their faces when they could play their first song, or sing and play at the same time, was wonderful. I gently encouraged them to sing along as I thought it would be good to learn that at the same time, and then hopefully it would not be so embarrassing for them later in life if they wanted to take guitar and singing into performing.

The other fortunate aspect of my group was that if someone needed a bit of a one-to-one for a short time, they were all very caring with one another and would practise while I gave some time to individuals.

What I learnt while teaching these children has thankfully stayed and has been used since to teach guitar on a one-to-one basis with two friends – one adult and one early teens – both very different people.

Singing in front of the children, teenagers and adults all those years ago gave me good grounding for what was to come later in life.

It was such an honour to sing at my friend's wedding; I also had the joy of singing at a wedding blessing. The Lord also brought into being my friend who can do mime. She is comfortable with me singing while she does this. We have both had the joy of doing this joint venture at her school, a nursing home and at afternoon talks.

Singing with friends is always a lovely experience; and again I was so happy when my friend gave me a chance to sing a real favourite song of mine. The night we were going to do this we ended up only having about twenty minutes to practise, and we had never sung together before. It had also been a long time since singing alone with a guy so I took a while to join in, but he was lovely and patient even though time was not on our side. When I did manage to join in we found our voices really complemented each other. So when it was our turn, we both got up and sang about the person we both have a relationship with and the aspect the Cross plays in that.

The song went down really well. I am so grateful to Jesus for all the good that has come out of the foundation He put into being all those years ago.

BLACK LEATHERS

In she comes – my friend dressed in her all-black leathers. She is someone I could look at without having to adjust my head as we were very similar in height. We didn't see a lot of each other, so in a way acquaintance is perhaps a word more suited, and yet, for the odd times we saw each other, we got on very well. She reminded me of the tomboy that has always been a part of the way I am.

Sometimes if she had time I would give her hair a trim followed by a wash and blow-dry, then catch-up time over a coffee for her and a cuppa for me, or sometimes a beer. One day she appeared out of nowhere. I had not seen her for probably over a year. My friend showed her in, still wearing her black leathers. I was so pleased to see her I nearly started to cry. She was not a person who liked to be hugged, which was fine by me, but that day she could see I was a bit overwhelmed and gave me a hug. During our conversation she asked if, as a thank-you to me for all the hair trims, coffee and beers, she could take me out for a ride on her bike. When we went outside I was astounded at the size of this motorbike considering her height and size. She was on in a flash, but it was my first experience of being on a motorbike, so with spare helmet securely fastened on my head I attempted to get on, accompanied by hysterical laughter from me and my friend. My little legs just seemed too short. How she kept the bike upright I will never know. I would get so far across, like when you do the splits and get stuck halfway. Still, we got there in the end, with our ribs hurting because of all the laughing.

Again I marvelled at how well she kept the bike up as at first I would lean too much when we went round corners. When we stopped at traffic lights this was gently mentioned, but then – blow me down! – I went the other way and did not lean enough. Bless her cotton socks, she gently mentioned this when we stopped to get some petrol. As I had had such a job getting on the bike we decided I should stay were I was; but I needed to keep still so she could get off with me and the bike still standing.

The expressions on the faces at the garage were a hoot. We both started to laugh but I soon realised I needed to hold it in, because when I was laughing it made the bike shake.

We then went out on the open road. It was brilliant and exhilarating. It was a fantastic afternoon. From a distance this young woman could alarm you – perhaps even scare you a little – and yet what you saw was only the style and colour of her clothes. The woman herself was down-to-earth, good company, and approachable.

Even though our time as friends was not overly long, the experience showed me how much I would have missed out if I had only gone on what my eyes were seeing rather than seeing the person.

COMMUNICATION

The day this friend showed up it had been a long time since we had seen each other. My surprise was that she had found me. The hair trims and coffee had always been at the flat where I lived with my husband. I no longer lived there and I had not seen her between the move and the change in my circumstances. As mentioned before, she had always been approachable and the day of the visit was no exception.

At this time I was living in a bedsit with a shared shower and toilet on the next floor, and the friend I was sharing with was a guy. By now I had lost most of my friends, and their willingness to still be my friend, but this woman did not scorn me.

Before the change in my circumstances I had become very lonely within the relationship with my husband. I felt that if I was the television I would have got much more attention. Communication had always been a *really* important part of our relationship right from the very beginning of our friendship, and all the way through right into our marriage. I watched the erosion of our communication with a deep sinking feeling in the pit of my stomach, and I *tried* to talk about it in the early stages of the erosion.

But you can't make someone listen; you can't change that person's ability to face what's going on if they don't want to face it. I am sure Jesus was trying to get his attention, but unfortunately we can close our hearts and minds to His nudging.

The guy I was now with had come down to spend time with his girlfriend. We were a pair of people who needed someone to listen. We needed to pray and try to understand the frustrations of struggling with relationships that we wanted to mend and that we were hoping our partners wanted to mend too. The sadness of not seeing it happen within our respective relationships did mean we cried on each other's shoulders.

Time went on with my husband and things did not improve. I had known people that had had nervous breakdowns and I knew the signs; I knew I was heading that way. Deep down I knew that if I stayed I would go under, so I moved out. This was not done lightly or without much soul-searching. I left a note in which I tried to explain in the best way I could why I had gone. When you're in turmoil it is admittedly not the best time to find the right words, but I had to try. I stayed with someone for a while. Sometimes you have to move again to save that precious relationship, and at the time it was the best thing for both of us. This is why I moved in with my friend.

Even though we both knew that our friendship had been innocent in the beginning of our individual problems, we knew that was not the case now.

Many, many years later I thought my husband and I were going to get back together. I was frightened, anxious, hopeful and intrigued all at the same time. I had gone to visit my dad and later that night waited outside the supermarket for my husband to pick me up so we could go for a drink. We got on very well and so followed visits to each other's towns to be with each other, and I got a chance to see his mum again, which was really nice.

Things were going so well that I was thinking of getting a transfer from my hospital to the one in my hometown, if it was possible, so we could be together. We talked about the breakdown in communication within our marriage and he was so sorry for the part he had played. He knew he was pushing me away and he could understand why I could not take any more. He was sorry that it had got to a point where I felt I had to go, but he could totally understand why I couldn't take any more. So there was sorry said by both of us for the pain given, and forgiveness asked and given to each other.

A few weeks later when he had not phoned I was getting worried. At the time I lived in a bedsit and my landlady didn't want me using the phone, because of the cost. I could understand this, and he had always been OK with it too, but that night I asked if I could use the phone as I was worried about him. The words that followed stunned me. When I did find my voice all I could say was, "What did you say?" It was made very clear, as mentioned further back in this book, that we would not be getting back together. The phone was just outside the landlady's sitting-room door. She came out to find me in a daze, and she said, "What on earth has he said to you?" When I told her, she took the phone off me and said exactly what she thought and put the phone down.

I crumpled to the floor in hysterical tears.

She was wonderful. We had become good friends, and she had taken time in the past to help me with English homework and had often looked after me if I'd been unwell. She nearly had to carry me upstairs to my room. I then curled up in the corner on my bed holding my pillow, and cried my heart out. She came in with a mug of tea. That night she slept on top of my bed with me in her arms, until I finally fell asleep with exhaustion. The next thing we knew the phone was ringing. It was my work. My landlady answered the phone and said I would not be in today. She then came upstairs with a cuppa to find me sobbing, as the memory of last night's phone call was the first thing that had come to mind as I was waking up.

She was so understanding and did not push me to eat. I really did not feel like eating, nor could I seem to stop crying. My, we got through a lot of tea that day! She will probably never know how much I owe her for helping me through that time. I did keep thanking her for the loving kindness she showed me; and I thanked Jesus for putting us together before it happened, and for our time together afterwards.

MY NEW MOTHER-IN-LAW

I remember my first Christmas with my new mother-in-law. She asked me what I would like for Christmas. At the time I was working as a nursing auxiliary on a long-stay elderly person's ward. The work was heavy and the shifts very tiring. I had always loved black-and-white films. My mother-in-law said there was a black-and-white version of *Pride and Prejudice* on the television over the Christmas period, so I said the best present for me would be to sit by the lovely coal fire watching my favourite film, which has always been *Pride and Prejudice* and which has two of my favourite actors – Laurence Olivier and Greer Garson.

So after work I went with my husband to visit his family. I was tired, so it was lovely to sit down in the car and rest my feet. When we arrived my mother-in-law gave me a lovely hug and as she did this I whispered, "Oh, Mum, I'm so tired. We were so busy at work."

She smiled at me and said, "Follow me." As we walked into their sitting room their coal fire was in full swing, so I sat down and made myself comfortable. The television had adverts on. Then a few minutes later she came in with a tray of tea, bread and butter, cakes, pickled onions, and a fork (for the onions). Then she gave the fire a poke, and, just before she left, *Pride and Prejudice* came on. My mouth dropped open. She just smiled and wished me a happy Christmas. Somehow she kept the rest of the family out so I could be left on my own to enjoy the film. Now and then she would come in quietly, refill the tray and leave.

I was so interested in the film that I did not notice the video machine was on record. She came back in and I thanked her for such a lovely, relaxing, peaceful, entertaining Christmas present.

The great thing was the fact that the film happened to be on when I could watch it and not miss it because of work. I came out of their sitting room refreshed, relaxed and grinning from ear to ear.

Then the icing on the cake was that just as we were leaving she gave me the video and said, "Now you can enjoy Laurence Olivier and his lovely high cheek bones and good looks without having to wait for it to come on at Christmas."

The thought and kindness that had gone into making that day very special for me was never forgotten.

Two very different ladies played different roles in where I was at the time, in my journey with life, Jesus, and friends. My *hope* was for both of them to see past me and somehow see Jesus despite my rough edges. And I hoped that Jesus would become as real to them as I know He can be if we let Him.

GAMES

I don't know about you, but I love receiving letters, cards and notes through the post. I love to sit in my favourite chair with a cuppa and curl up and enjoy them.

How time changes things!

Now and then I would get an invitation to a party, which sometimes would mean getting dressed up. This was OK, but given the choice the tomboy in me would at times rather not have done. The little girl in me who wanted to dress up and the tomboy part of me were often in conflict, even though this was never shown on the outside.

The parties often consisted of games (oh no!). The only one I liked was pass the parcel. It's sad – I still do. It was such a strange feeling because I sort of wanted the parcel to stop with me, and yet I hoped it wouldn't at the same time. Then as I grew older the games seemed to get even stranger, like sucking peas through a straw from one bowl to another. The winner was the one to put the most peas in the empty bowl.

The friend's house where this and other games were played was gigantic. You could have used the sitting room as a car showroom. As we walked up to this house, in all honesty I felt a little intimidated. When we got inside, this house also had at least three bathrooms and three to four toilets. This was unusual at the time.

I remember my relief when the games stopped and we went downstairs for drinks and food (yippee!). While we fed our faces my friend and her mum did some rock-and-roll jiving. This was more like it! After a while we all got up and had a go. The best bit was jiving with my friend. She was really good and coped well when now and then I would accidentally switch to ballroom jive – the two are quite different. After a while I needed to go to the toilet, got lost, found one, came out, got lost, and then in my travels to get back to the jiving I passed a room with the door ajar. I peeped through the gap and saw a bathroom off to the side of a bedroom. I thought 'Wow!' and I'm ashamed to say inquisitiveness got the better of me. I went and had a look, and then felt guilty for being so nosey.

I was not in a relationship with Jesus at this time and so things through the post did not always bring me the pleasure that would have been intended by the friend. However, sometimes to show your vulnerability to the age group that you are a part of can be one of the hardest things to do, whether the age group you're in be children, teens, or adults.

I was to find out later that, whether your personality is assertive or not, your desire to say yes to Jesus is really the punchline.

PUNCHLINE

This lady was the sister of my dear Jucos teacher. She was tall and her facial features, including hair, eyes and complexion, were quite different to those of her sister. She was quite assertive, but not in a nasty way. There was an elegance about her. She would wear clothes that flowed and had movement. When she walked into a room her presence was endearing and yet strong and bold. You could sense her assertive personality. She was strong, bold, astounding, astute; she seemed confident and yet shy; she was quite attractive, and could be formidable.

She was a professional opera singer and sang in front of audiences that could be vast, with an orchestra to accompany her, or at smaller venues with a piano or organ.

Now and then when she was not working she would sing at the little church her sister and I attended. I remember the organist would get excited as it gave him a chance to play music that was more difficult – which he was very capable of doing. I would look at her and think, 'I don't think you need a mike.'

This lady said yes to the free gift that Jesus was offering, which was Himself, and which she knew opened up for her a relationship with Father God, as well as a relationship with Jesus.

To enter into a relationship with Father God and Jesus, along with her sister, my lovely teacher, was the choice she made – not because she needed a crutch, not because she was unintelligent, not because she was assertive. These were her quirks – bits of her personality. Jesus didn't take away these characteristics, but enhanced the person she was. She became His voice, hands and feet. She said yes to this amazing person who laid down His life. By saying yes she knew she would not be cut off from Father God any more.

ICE SKATING

We can be cut off from all sorts of things: places, people, interest, family, relationships and many more. People are like Liquorice Allsorts or a box of Cadbury's Roses: we all come in different shapes, sizes, characteristics and temperaments. So, because of this, some people you glide along with and with others it might be a little more problematic for both of you.

Apart from dancing, when I was young and growing towards my teens, my other interest was ice skating. If it came on the television, I loved to watch the competitors skating in couples or on their own.

Sadly we did not live near an ice rink, but that did not stop the thoughts of wanting to ice-skate for my own country. Distances cut us off from pursuing this avenue long-term. However, one day my dad took me and my sister to an ice rink. It had a smaller beginners' rink and a larger one for the more accomplished.

In the car I could hardly control my excitement. I probably didn't. For once, being short had its advantages – well, that's what I hoped for. My thinking was that I wouldn't have so far to fall, so it wouldn't hurt so much. My! this is so not true.

We started on the beginners' rink with me clinging on for dear life. Unfortunately there were little gaps in the sides so people could get on and off the rink. The fear factor would triple but you had to try and get across, otherwise a queue would build up behind you.

At this particular rink there were some helpers who would come and try to encourage you to leave the side – that's if they could convince you and your hand to let go. If I didn't, the helper said, I would cut myself off from having a go and enjoying the freedom of skating. Try telling my legs that! But of course she was right. So off we went with me hanging onto her. With every wobble my heart went into my mouth. I thought she must be able to hear my heart – it sounded like an amplified bass drum and felt like it could burst out of my chest at any moment.

It was awe-inspiring that she could keep me and herself upright, even though to start with my legs had other ideas. But slowly my confidence grew and I had a go on my own. I was very grateful for her patience and understanding.

I seemed to be doing OK, and then people changed direction.

'Oh, man,' I thought, 'you must be joking! I've only just got used to going this way and sort of staying up.' So the inevitable had to happen: down I went. My! hard ice and a bony bottom do not go well together.

The person who had helped me came to my aid and said, "Don't let the discomfort of the fall cut you off from getting up and trying again."

I don't know about discomfort – more like ouch! – but she was right, so up I got and tried again.

After a while I plucked up courage and thought, 'I'll have a go on the big rink.' Well, that was once I had mastered staying upright while trying to come to a stop. And then I had to master walking on skates where the surface is rubber with small ridges on it, without catching those ridges with the slim metal bar that was part of my boot.

My! what a sight to behold!

I was very slim, and when I wobbled out came my arms to help me balance. Up to this point I hadn't seen anyone fall while getting from one rink to another. I thought 'My! if I fall while trying to achieve the same as everyone else, I'll never live it down.'

I managed to get there in one piece. What a relief! I'm not sure if my outstretched arms took anyone out. I hope not.

When I made it to the big rink I must admit the urge to go back to the side was strong. Off I went, thinking, 'Thank goodness we are all going the same way!'

There were people in the centre of the rink doing awe-inspiring things, but I found out quite quickly you can't watch them and what you're doing without consequences (falling on my bony bottom).

We went home bruised, cold and a little damp.

The one-off visit was brilliant, but the distance made further visits difficult. However, with a lot of encouragement from the helper at the rink that day, the ouch did not cut me off from having a wonderful afternoon.

As time went by, the happy memories of that afternoon helped me to come to terms with the realisation that I would never be a serious ice skater.

And thanks, Dad, for taking us that day. You must have been frozen.

DOORS

Sin separates us from God. Some people might not be troubled about this, but we all have a conscience, and it is our choice whether we listen, acknowledge, and care that it might be pricking, urging us about whatever. And free will was also given to us.

I remember a lady I met at a weekend away; she was the other half of the speaker at this particular event. This comparative stranger, who like me was not overly tall and had a bright, bubbly, jolly personality, was very spiritual but at the same time extremely approachable.

I was having a chat with her and her husband in private, and she mentioned that puppets are controlled by someone pulling on different strings to make them react to the music or a script.

Our precious free will, along with our consciences, were given to us so we respond or not to Father God and Jesus.

Once you stop moving the strings of a puppet, they are lifeless. By giving us free will the strings are removed and we choose to accept Jesus and welcome Him into our lives and hearts or not. Father God does not want puppets that have to be controlled by a hand or string. For us to come – to *want* to come – on our own accord is great.

By giving us free will there is always the possibility of Him being rejected!

Most doors have a handle on both sides so you have a choice to open and go in, or have to wait for a person to let you in. Walking into a crowded room on your own can be quite daunting, especially if you don't know anyone, or if the one person you do know has not yet arrived.

I spent quite a few years on my own and did not always have someone whom I could walk into a room with. This episode is a prime example. I decided to go to college and have a go at City and Guilds in English, and have a go at some maths too. So off I went to enrol. Well, as you've probably realised, I am renowned for getting lost. There seemed to be endless corridors with every subject under the sun except the one I was looking for. I was so relieved when I found it. I didn't notice that I had entered the class without thinking about it – well, not until I realised everyone was looking up from their tables to see who had walked in. However, a lovely lady gave me a big warm smile and happened to be available, which made a world of difference. We had a lovely chat, and before leaving I was extremely glad to know she would be the teacher for the English course I was to participate in.

English was taught in a good-size prefab that was sat with other buildings of the same kind on the playground. It was quite dark, apart from the lights coming from the buildings.

The first night of the English course arrived, and, even though I knew the lovely teacher would be there, the thought of walking into this room of complete strangers was daunting. As I was walking towards the prefab I noticed it was a full class. Twice I bottled out. If anyone had seem me from outside they could have wondered what I was doing. I would go up and look through the window and if anyone turned my way I would bob down out of sight. Well, they only had to turn their heads towards the window and I would bob down out of the way. I would then make sure no one could see me and quickly walk back to my bike.

The third time I went I got through the door and stood in the gap that was between two doors. One led into City and Guilds and the other Royal Society of Arts in English language. This time I didn't move quickly enough and was seen. I was just about to make a dash for it when the teacher came out and intervened.

You know what it's like when you walk into a room – people naturally look up to see who has come in. In the meantime you're very much aware that your face is red enough to cook a fried egg on each cheek. Also every time I went I knew I should have got there before it started or on time. Well, you could say that about anything that means you've got to walk into a room. However, the making of friends does improve matters.

The teacher opened the door and encouraged me to join the rest of the class. The door to our souls only has a handle on one side –

inside. Jesus will try and reach you, like He used my friend to reach me so that I could relate to what He was offering (Himself).

My teacher opened the door into the class and I had a few seconds to decide whether to go through or not.

Because the handle, so to speak, is one way, only you can open it; whereas the door that has a handle on both sides means you might go in, though not always with complete agreement from your whole being. When you open the door of your soul (heart) to Jesus it's done with freedom of mind, body and soul.

HORSE RIDING

Many, many years ago I had a go at horse riding. I have always liked animals, my favourites being dolphins, elephants and horses. I think the shire horses are magnificent; I have always thought of them as gentle giants.

Being a novice at riding I was given a horse that was used for new riders. The horses certainly came in all shapes and sizes, a bit like the people riding them.

My riding hat was very important – it saved my head from serious injury many a time. To begin with, even though I was taught how to encourage my horse to turn left, right, trot, and gallop, achieving this was quite hard.

Ducking came in handy to start with, when a sturdy branch was sticking out and I couldn't quite convince my horse to go round. The trouble was that sometimes I would come up too early and get smacked in the face by the next branch. Or there would be bushes that were very wide. I would find this out as I would lean away, over-lean, and the ground and I would come together again.

There were two grey horses at this riding school and they were lovely – very majestic. When I first started I thought I would love to ride them one day.

The day came and, when I looked in the register, by my name was the name of one of the grey horses. My first ride with him was quite an experience. He was very energetic and curious. If something was going on at the front of the group and he was at the back, before you could stop him he was there. As I became more used to him things improved, but he was always quite a handful.

The other grey horse was so completely different. He was very calm and peaceful, but he had a problem with sneezing (bless him!). In the summer when it was dusty this made it worse for him so when we went into a trot or gallop he would sneeze his way through this activity. My heart went out to him. He still stayed calm and was a joy to ride and be with.

I didn't always have the physical strength or riding skills to instruct the more energetic grey horse to do what the rest of the group were doing or to get him to wait his turn. His enthusiasm was so strong, and I just was not overkeen on using the whip. He was brilliant to be with, even if you did feel worn out after being with him.

I cared about them both. They were so similar in height and colour and yet so different. The calmer one I called Sneezes. They both brought different strengths and characteristics out of my personality and showed me things about myself that could be improved. I am so grateful that I had the opportunity to care for two very special horses.

LOVING

It is hard to care for someone when every part of your being is saying no, when your mind and emotions are thinking I cannot bear the pain, rejection, hurt and injustices that are being dished out again.

To care for an animal can be so much easier. Their love tends to be unrestricted, uncomplicated and unbiased.

Thank goodness for friends who come into our journey of life; who try to love us with an understanding that there might be failure on both sides; who try to love unconditionally.

Along with loving, caring and allowing people to care for you, there is a common thread that at some point in each human's life there will come a physical, emotional, mental, even spiritual difficulty whether small, medium or large (not said lightly), along with joy.

On a cold December morning I was walking behind a lady and her little girl. As they turned the corner the bright Christmas lights sparkled in the dimness. The little girl let out a cry of delight. Her joy, pleasure and excitement changed my perception, and I found myself sharing her delight. I was still smiling when I got home. These two people were totally unaware of how the little girl's spontaneity refreshed me and others that were around at the time. Perhaps it proves the point that sometimes we grow up too soon?

I heard a wise person once say, "I would not ask you to do what I myself had not done first." This was mentioned in a work sense; however, it could be quite applicable to many situations in life.

If you have got this far in this book you will have realised that sadly I have caused pain and been on the receiving end also. The difference has been having help from the inside out, along with amazing friends and family.

And for the people who have few friends or no family, or who have personal experiences of being a round peg in a square hole and all that goes with that, I know Jesus understands because it happened to Him.

One reason Jesus didn't fit in (round peg in a square hole) was because He was willing to do all that His Heavenly Father desired of Him. That did not always fit in with what the culture was at that time; nor did it fit in with the community where He lived, or later as He moved further afield.

He loved and valued and showed just as much respect and fairness to the women as to the children and men. This would have been frowned on. Religious ideology was not high on His list, which again did not always sit well with some people He came into contact with.

Being real, using short stories about life to get a point across was an important way for Him to communicate with people. They listened to what was said and decided whether to act upon it or not. He was interested in individuals as well as the group, making no distinction between class or colour.

Showing the opposite response to what people expected Him to do, say, think, and feel came at a cost. The cost was sometimes that He seemed mysterious; He was ridiculed, unwanted, scoffed at, jeered, unappreciated and misunderstood.

There was a lady I worked with many years ago. We had both undergone ear operations and earache and pain. When I went to work and had earache my other work colleagues showed concern. Their sincerity was real, but because this lady had experienced the pain there was a fellow-feeling between us.

Jesus' ability to understand how it feels to be spoken to in an unkind manner is real, as mentioned above.

This is not a study/theological/theatrical book. It's a book about the thirty-three years Father God and Jesus have spent together with me, along with the important part the Holy Spirit has played in that time. This is about getting to know someone. Father God was separated from us because sin entered the arena (Genesis). Jesus came to live on earth, so He understands us; He understands me. He took on Himself my sin, the stuff that separates me from the holiness of Father God. He died an *agonising* death; He defeated death by rising.

There is nothing wrong with being academic, but with a deep sense of security I know I am not. I do not have the answers to a lot of things.

You choose whether to acknowledge the gift being offered to you by Father God (Jesus). You choose whether to ask Him into your heart and life. You choose whether to acknowledge the sin that is always trying to do the complete opposite and keep you as far away as possible from the truth that God sent and that Jesus is offering. You can chose to be more courageous and not join in with a group that is picking on another. It was not always the case, but a lot of the times I was teased it was more likely to be by a group. It was as though they needed the encouragement of each other.

A person who has learnt that fireworks can hurt will urge others to be more careful. Making mistakes is part of life. In love we don't insist – we *urge* someone not to go down that road because we want to spare them the pain. We endeavour to urge, share and communicate as best we can.

Even though there are different versions of the Bible, I personally believe it to be the Word of God and still extremely helpful.

The essence of the content is still the same, whichever translation you decide to have a nose at or jump right in there and read.

It's a bit like the old classic films. They have been done more than once, the difference being colour instead of black-and-white, or the actors and actresses may put their styles into the part they're playing, but the essence of the film is still the same.

Different churches have different styles. If you're shy or have a quiet personality it may not suit you to go to one that is big (lots of people), or loud and energetic in its praise and worship. God loves variety. You've only got to watch a gardening programme to see how much variety was created.

Personally I think it's rather neat – after all, we're all different and that includes how we may wish to worship or which style of teaching we prefer.

Sorry, but I've got to say it again – the essence is still whom you're worshipping and whom you're learning more about!

I love sixties' music and will choose a seat at the back so the only thing I could upset is the wall. There will be a strong possibility that it won't be long before I will be up dancing. We've all gone to see the same group and listened to the same music, but some will be up, and some will stay seated for all or part of it, etc.

SAD – HAPPY

There is often sad news on the television because of the way people have treated one another and the ripple effect that has. Or we hear about the ups and downs of the lives of celebrities. I sometimes wonder if they would like their working and personal lives to be much more separate issues?

The following are things that may never make the news or appear in a magazine, but which can form a golden thread weaving its way through our lives:

A sunset or sunrise that has colours in it that make you swell inside at the sight you're beholding; a lake that has a reflection of breathtaking scenery; a cathedral that has awesome stonework on the outside and inside a cool, calm peacefulness that can help to still you, especially if you're all hot and bothered. A park can also be a quiet oasis from the noise of a city or the business of the town.

A smile from a stranger may make a world of difference. There's a pathway I sometimes follow that leads onto a housing estate. On this pathway there are a few bungalows. When I use my bike or walk along this path, if there is someone standing and looking through one of the windows, I see the difference a wave and a smile can make. Their faces light up. Even with a gate or window between us it means only a few monuments to say hi with body language rather than words, and we are both left with smiles on our faces. I always get a smile, wave or both back.

Icicles can be stunning if the light catches them; the face of a child the first time she or he sees pretty lights lit; a rainbow arching across the sky on a grey day; laughter that makes your ribs ache; the fun and exasperation of miniature golf; the smallness of a ladybird; the largeness of a whale; a blossom tree bearing beautiful shades of purple, pink and white; when you're fortunate to have neighbours that are also your friends; the joy of a well and the clean water that will come out of it for the people of that community; a voice that when listened to makes the hair on your skin stand up or gives you goose pimples.

All these things can bring joy. Even if they be for a moment they can so easily be missed.

LIFE

A passport if not packed can cause great stress; without it, travelling in business class, first class or economy class would make no difference. That passport is the key to your being able to continue your journey and get home again.

Just as it's your choice to believe whether there is a Heaven and Hell, you have the choice to reject or accept the gift that Jesus is offering – Himself.

There are many types of apples, with different sizes, colours and tastes, but when they have been eaten we are all left with the same thing – a core.

A crack in a wall can be small, and yet if left untreated it can become bigger and then need more rubbing down, more time and more plastering.

A smile or a hug, the squeeze of a hand, or tears are part of a universal language. There need be no barrier of not being able to speak the language of another person, whether in spoken words or sign language.

To be loved is also a universal need. Your age, height, colour, size and background are all part of your individuality along with a desire, a need, to be loved. Changes come into our lives and affect our ability to love or be loved. However, there is still a fundamental basis that love can and does achieve more than we could know or ever understand.

Poor reasons, such as weariness, can stop me allowing Jesus to shine His beauty forth day and night. My restlessness wouldn't let my mind rest. Lord, please be my off button.

The snowdrops were bent over. Some stood tall, some unsure. Jesus, I can be like that. (Can you?) You bend over and give me an invisible hug or stand by me with quiet love. You are with us in our in-betweens. Thank You.

As I walk through the allotment, the trees are silent, bare, looking forlorn, and yet inside they quietly wait to surge forth. There's a tree that's large, beautiful, bare and yet alive, waiting to show its astounding beauty, to shout, "You see, I'm alive. My season has come."

There was a season, a right time, to write my first little book, and then there was a season for the second book. Sometimes I (we) can be like that tree. It may or may not be the right time for you to read this book, but thank you for reading it anyway. And whatever season you may be in now, may I invite you to talk to Jesus and allow Him into your winter, spring, summer and autumn.